INSPIRATION

IMAGES OF JESUS

A Spiral Coloring Book *for* Christians

Jonathan Alexander Scott

DEDICATION

For you and all your secret or forgotten creativity.

CONTENTS

SPIRAL COLORING

Spiral coloring is a meditative technique that involves coloring intricate patterns, often featuring spirals as a central element. While spiral coloring is often associated with mindfulness and relaxation, it is also a powerful tool for Christian prayer and meditation.

Spiral coloring can be helpful in Christian prayer by serving as a visual aid for meditation. Many people find it difficult to sit still and quiet their mind during prayer, but focusing on the intricate patterns and colors of a spiral coloring page can provide a point of focus for the mind. This helps calm the mind and creates a more peaceful, meditative state, which is always beneficial for prayer and reflection.

In addition to serving as a visual aid for meditation, spiral coloring can also be a great way to explore Christian themes and symbols. Coloring these designs can help to deepen your understanding and connection to these symbols and their significance in your faith.

Another way spiral coloring can be helpful in Christian prayer is by promoting a sense of creativity and self-expression. By coloring intricate designs and experimenting with different color combinations, you will be free to explore your own creativity and express yourself in a unique and personal way. This can be a powerful tool for prayer and reflection, as it allows you to explore your thoughts, feelings, and beliefs in a creative and expressive way.

Finally, spiral coloring can be a great way to promote relaxation and reduce stress, which I great for prayer and meditation. By focusing on the process of coloring and allowing the mind to relax, you will create a more peaceful and calm state, which is truly conducive to prayer and reflection.

Spiral coloring is a powerful tool for Christian prayer and meditation. By serving as a visual aid for meditation, exploring Christian themes and symbols, promoting creativity and self-expression, and promoting relaxation and stress reduction, spiral coloring can help to deepen your connection to your faith and create a more peaceful and meditative state.

HOW TO USE THIS BOOK

Here are some simple instructions to get you started:

1. Choose your supplies:

    All you will need is this spiral coloring book, colored pencils, markers or crayons, and a comfortable space to color.

2. Choose your design:

    Look through your coloring book and choose a design that appeals to you.

3. Choose your colors:

    Select the colors you want to use for your design. You can use one color for the entire design, or choose a variety of colors to create a more complex and interesting design.

4. Start coloring:

    Begin coloring your design, starting at the center and working your way outwards. Take your time and focus on coloring each section of the design carefully and thoughtfully. Use light pressure for a softer look, or press harder for a bolder effect.

5. Add details: Once you have colored the main sections of your design, you can add details such as shading or highlights to create depth and dimension.

6. Relax and enjoy:

    Take your time and enjoy the process of coloring. Spiral coloring is a great way to relax and unwind, so read the verse, take deep breaths and let your mind think about the verse as you color.

Remember, there are no rules when it comes to spiral coloring. It's all about having fun and expressing yourself through color and design.

So go ahead and let your creativity flow!

For God so loved the world that he gave his one and only Son, that whoever believes in him shall not perish but have eternal life.

John 3:16

The Word became flesh and made his dwelling among us. We have seen his glory, the glory of the one and only Son, who came from the Father, full of grace and truth.

John 1:14

Then Jesus declared, 'I am the bread of life. Whoever comes to me will never go hungry, and whoever believes in me will never be thirsty.'

John 6:35

I am the way and the truth and the life. No one comes to the Father except through me.'

John 14:6

I am the resurrection and the life. The one who believes in me will live, even though they die.

John 11:25

For the wages of sin is death, but the gift of God is eternal life in Christ Jesus our Lord.

Romans 6:23

Therefore, if anyone is in Christ, the new creation has come: The old has gone, the new is here!

2 Corinthians 5:17

In him we have redemption through his blood, the forgiveness of sins, in accordance with the riches of God's grace.

Ephesians 1:7

Let us then approach God's throne of grace with confidence, so that we may receive mercy and find grace to help us in our time of need.

Hebrews 4:16

But God demonstrates his own love for us in this: While we were still sinners, Christ died for us.

Romans 5:8

I am the vine; you are the branches. If you remain in me and I in you, you will bear much fruit; apart from me you can do nothing.

John 15:5

I have been crucified with Christ and I no longer live, but Christ lives in me. The life I now live in the body, I live by faith in the Son of God, who loved me and gave himself for me.

Galatians 2:20

In your relationships with one another, have the same mindset as Christ Jesus: Who, being in very nature God, did not consider equality with God something to be used to his own advantage; rather, he made himself nothing by taking the very nature of a servant, being made in human likeness. And being found in appearance as a man, he humbled himself by becoming obedient to death—even death on a cross!

Philippians 2:5-10

Therefore he is able to save completely those who come to God through him, because he always lives to intercede for them.

Hebrews 7:25

This is how God showed his love among us: He sent his one and only Son into the world that we might live through him. This is love: not that we loved God, but that he loved us…

1 John 4:9-10

For what I received I passed on to you as of first importance: that Christ died for our sins according to the Scriptures, that he was buried, that he was raised on the third day according to the Scriptures.

1 Corinthians 15:3-4

But we do see Jesus, who was made lower than the angels for a little while, now crowned with glory and honor because he suffered death, so that by the grace of God he might taste death for everyone.

Hebrews 2:9

I am the light of the world. Whoever follows me will never walk in darkness, but will have the light of life.

John 8:12

If we confess our sins, he is faithful and just and will forgive us our sins and purify us from all unrighteousness.

1 John 1:9

I am the Alpha and the Omega,' says the Lord God, 'who is, and who was, and who is to come, the Almighty.

Revelation 1:8

For I am convinced that neither death nor life, neither angels nor demons, neither the present nor the future, nor any powers, neither height nor depth, nor anything else in all creation, will be able to separate us from the love of God that is in Christ Jesus our Lord.

Romans 8:38-39

And this is the testimony: God has given us eternal life, and this life is in his Son. Whoever has the Son has life…

1 John 5:11-12

For the message of the cross is foolishness to those who are perishing, but to us who are being saved it is the power of God.

1 Corinthians 1:18

Salvation is found in no one else, for there is no other name under heaven given to mankind by which we must be saved.

Acts 4:12

God was pleased to have all his fullness dwell in him, and through him to reconcile to himself all things, whether things on earth or things in heaven, by making peace through his blood, shed on the cross.

Colossians 1:20

Therefore, there is now no condemnation for those who are in Christ Jesus.

Romans 8:1

I am the good shepherd. The good shepherd lays down his life for the sheep.

John 10:11

For it is by grace you have been saved through faith, and this is not from yourselves, it is the gift of God—
not by works, so that no one can boast.

Ephesians 2:8-9

I am the Alpha and the Omega, the First and the Last, the Beginning and the End.

Revelation 22:13

Worthy is the Lamb, who was slain, to receive power and wealth and wisdom and strength and honor and glory and praise!

Revelation 5:12

More Books in This Series

I hope you have enjoyed using these designs to reflect on who Jesus is.

I hope they have stilled your mind and quieted your heart to hear what God is saying.

If you would like to discover more books like this, please go to https://geni.us/inspirationbooks to find more books in this series so you can feel more peace as you get closer to God.

Or scan this code with your phone to be taken straight to the Amazon page where you can choose your next book.

The translations of the Bible verses in this book are taken from different versions including the New International Version (NIV), English Standard Version (ESV), New Living Translation (NLT), and the King James Version (KJV).